for all partners in this collective work-in-progress

Vyzoviti, Sophia
Supersurfaces: Folding as a method of generating forms for architecture, products and fashion

BIS Publishers
Herengracht 370-372
P.O. Box 323
1000 AH Amsterdam
The Netherlands
T 00 31 (0)20 5247560
F 00 31 (0)20 5247557
www.bispublishers.nl
bis@bispublishers.nl

ISBN 90 6369 121 1

BIS

contents

The 'triangulating' category includes flat-state patterns of arrays of equilateral or isosceles triangles. Here, three-dimensionality is achieved by creasing along the triangle vertices with alternating concave and convex creases, transforming the flat plane into a double-corrugated surface. Triangulated paperfolds share the property of inextensional folding – that is, they can be packaged flat. According to Pellegrino and Vincent,[6] 'inextensional folding requires that whenever different creases meet at a common point there should be at least four folds, of which three have one sign (convex or concave) and one fold has the opposite sign (concave or convex).'

The category of 'crumpling' includes flat-state patterns of random crease lines and irregular facets. Crumpling is a gesture of minimum effort/maximum three-dimensional effect, explicated here by the operations: crease, press and wrap.

Paperfolds are manipulable: bendable, flexible, versatile and retractable. Some are able to deploy themselves, expanding and contracting. Some achieve a number of equilibrium states upon a plane, balancing in different positions. Some retrieve several shapes, adjusting to their context. The versatile and polymorphic nature of paperfolds increases their potential to generate design prototypes. The investigation of ways to make paperfolds productive within a hands-on and process-driven design methodology of form generation is coupled with explorations into material behavior and usability. Paperfold algorithms can be executed on alternative surface materials: foam, rubber, pvc, polypropylene, polyethelene, re-enforced fabrics, gypsum band, mesh, leather, copper, aluminum or plywood. Scaling up paper into larger, thicker, stiffer and waterproof surfaces instigates inventive responses in terms of size, usage, texture and structure.

Transcribing the intrinsic properties of paperfolds into the development of prototypes enables improvisations with a wide range of applicability. Oscillating between the micro and the macro scale, supersurfaces engage a design field that is a fusion between architecture, interior, product and fashion. Overall, the design prototypes presented in *Supersurfaces* correspond to Mollerup's definition of the 'collapsible', an umbrella term he invented for a number of everyday objects that 'fold out for action and fold up for storage'[7]. The series of possible applications presented here includes playthings, ornaments, garments, furniture, furnishings, and architectural components. Partially resolved, potentially implementable, these emergent prototypes maintain their diagrammatic quality. They abstain from the exactitude of technical drawing, indulging into the affinity of directed indeterminacy.

While not bound by a linear form of logic, the development of paperfolds into potential objects and spaces is practiced methodically: intuitive paper-folding session, sufficient description of generative pattern and algorithm, family of objects, comprehension of intrinsic properties and transcription of those properties towards a prototype within a fusion design field. As a design method, supersurfaces is agnostic, experimental, improvisational and liberating, and is fundamentally a diagrammatic technique.[8] As a counterpart to present-day overriding research into the 'genetics of form' through computer-aided design and manufacturing, supersurfaces can be appreciated as a 'low tech-high concept'[9] approach – a radical/retro practice: hands-on, process-driven design methodology. Despite its analogue constitution, supersurfaces is an intelligent design method, engaging basic-level computation, relying essentially on brainware (and handware) rather than software.

references

1 See also: Vyzoviti, S., *Folding Architecture - Concise Genealogy of the Practice in Folding Architecture: Spatial, structural and organizational diagrams* (Amsterdam, BIS Publishers, 2003)

2 Relationships between the notions of surface, folding, unfolding, topology, land strategy, systems and devices, as well as paradoxes, origami, bends and unbendings, braids, coiling, contortionisms are elucidated in Gauza M. et al, *The Metapolis dictionary of advanced architecture* (Barcelona, Actar, 2003).

3 Developable surfaces are surfaces that can be flattened to a plane without tearing or stretching; examples include the cylinder, the cone, and the torus. See http://en.wikipedia.org/wiki/Surface

4 This is a basic level definition of algorithm: A finite set of well-defined rules for the solution of a problem in a finite number of steps. An algorithm (the word is derived from the name of the Persian mathematician Al-Khwarizmi), is a finite set of well-defined instructions for accomplishing some task which, given an initial state, will terminate in a corresponding recognizable end-state (contrast with heuristic). See http://en.wikipedia.org/wiki/Algorithm

5 The category is named by analogy to the 'ruled surface'. In geometry, a surface S is ruled if through every point of S there is a straight line that lies on S. See http://en.wikipedia.org/wiki/Ruled_surface

6 Pellegrino, S. and Vincent, J., 'How to fold a membrane' in *Deployable Structures*, ed. Pelligrino, S. (SpringerWienNewYork, 2001)

7 Mollerup, P., *Collapsibles: a design album of space saving objects.* (London, Thames and Hudson, 2001)

8 The prime advantages of the diagrammatic technique, according to Van Berkel and Boss, is liberation from architectural typology and the introduction of 'qualities that are disconnected from an ideal or an ideology, random, intuitive and subjective'. Van Berkel and Boss, in *Move: Techniques: network spin* (Amsterdam, Goose Press, 1999)

9 By analogy to Stan Allen's 'low-definition, high-concept' versus the 'high-definition, low-concept' in Allen, S., 'The Digital Complex' in *Log*, volume 5

elastic paper band

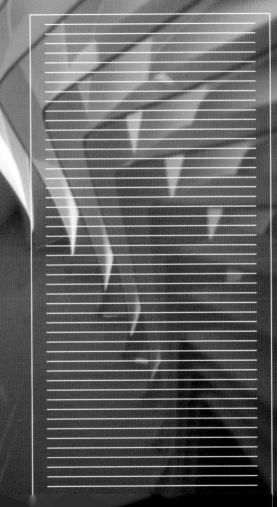

[rule-cut-bloat-fold-unfold-stretch]

bloat

fold

2.   lanternette

14

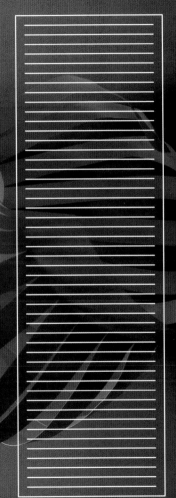

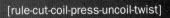
[rule-cut-coil-press-uncoil-twist]

coil

press

spread

twist

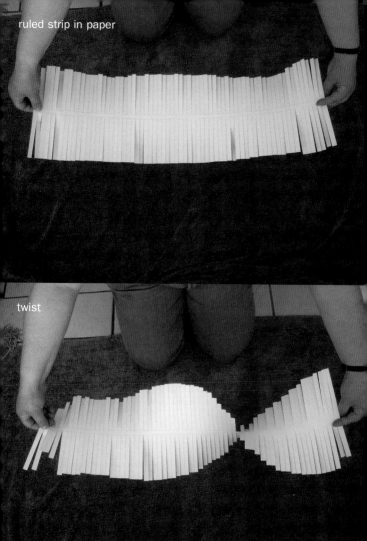

ruled strip in paper

twist

helix edges

wrap

23

helix edges

wrap

ruled strip in rubber

twist

24

twister in rubber

assemble by interspacing

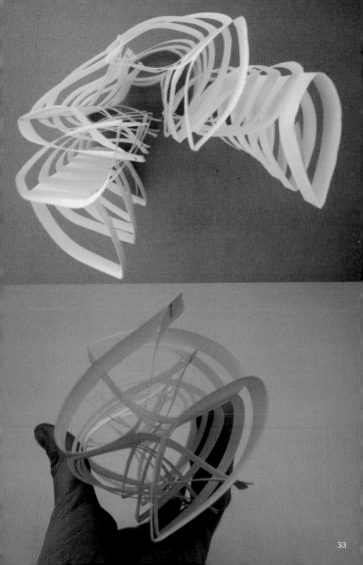

cardboard

cork

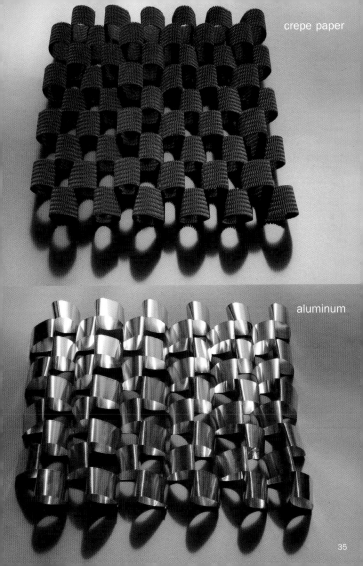

crepe paper

aluminum

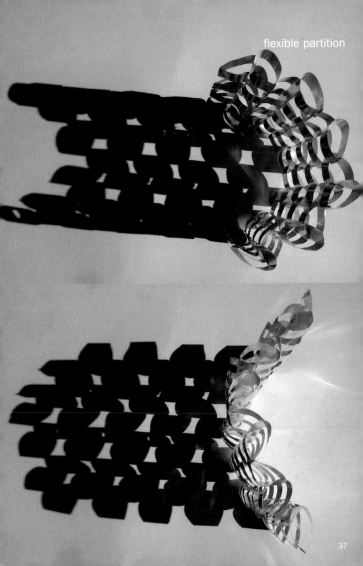

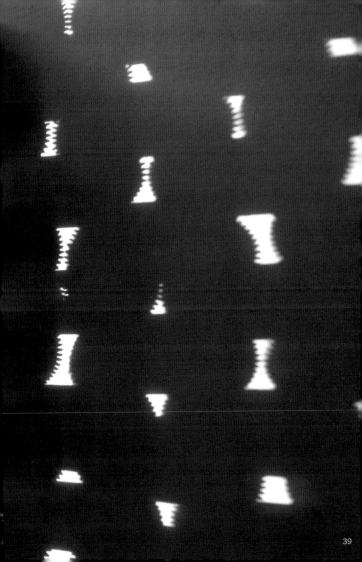

5.   flexichair

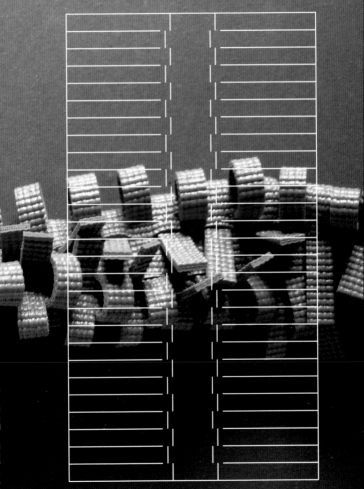

[rule-cut-rotate-pierce]

self-intersecting strip in paper

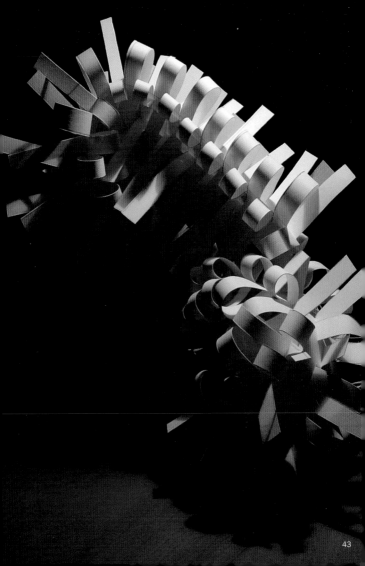

self-intersecting strip in rubber

self-intersecting strip in polyethelene

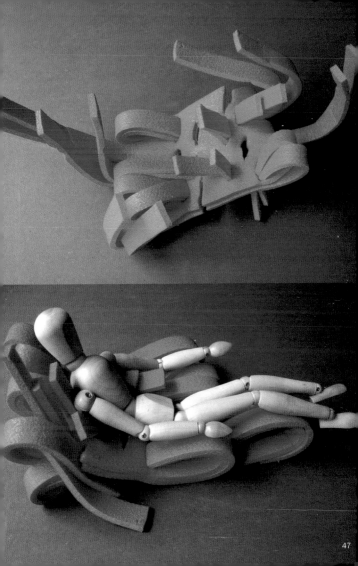

flexichair

6.   body wraps

[rule-cut-rotate-pierce]

cardboard   polypropylene

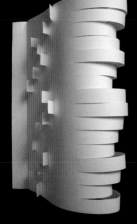
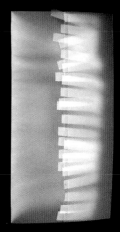

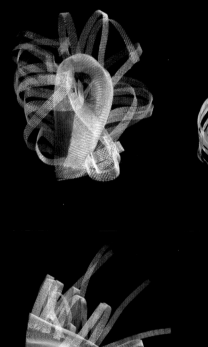

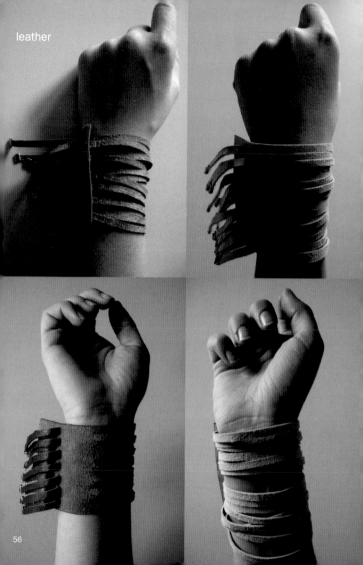

leather

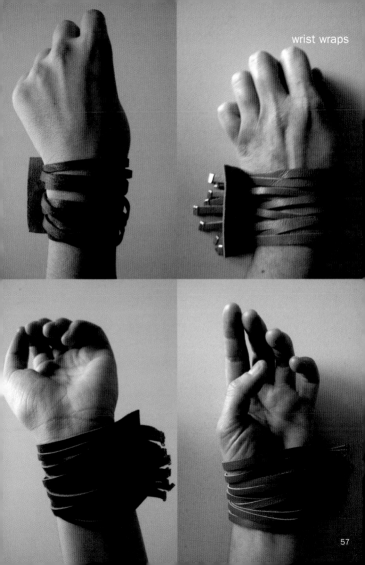

7. body donuts

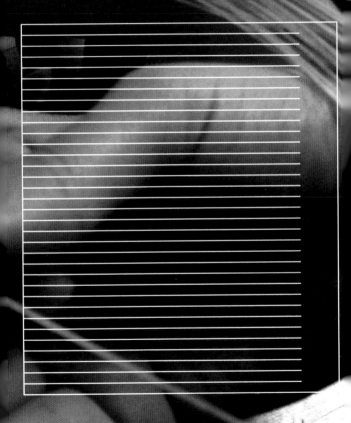

paper

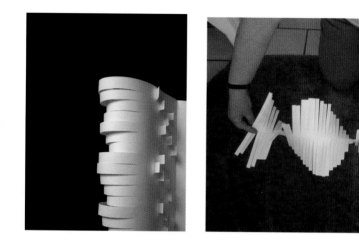

torus [annulus revolved clockwise]

annulus [rule-cut-coil]

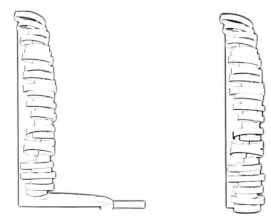

torus [annulus revolved counterclockwise]

reinforced foam

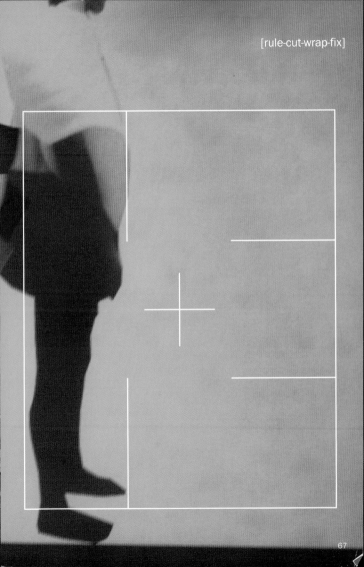

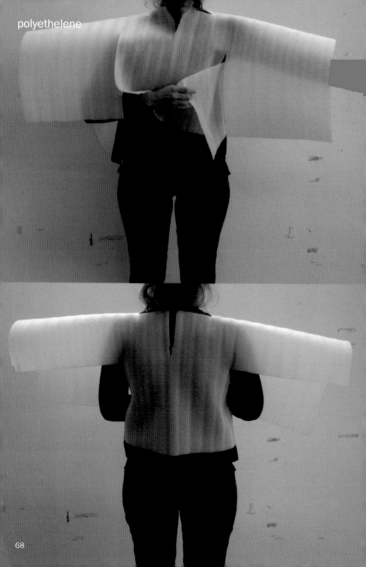

polyethelene

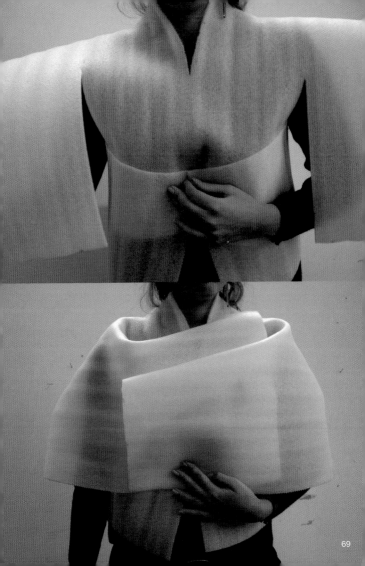

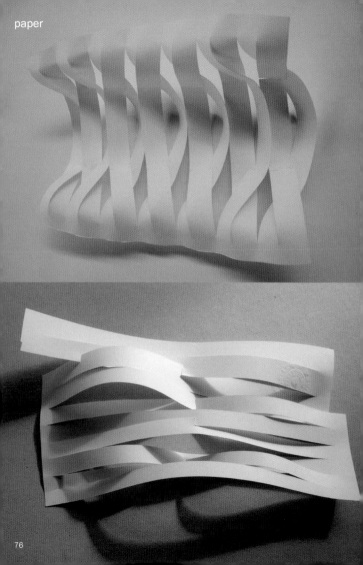

plywood

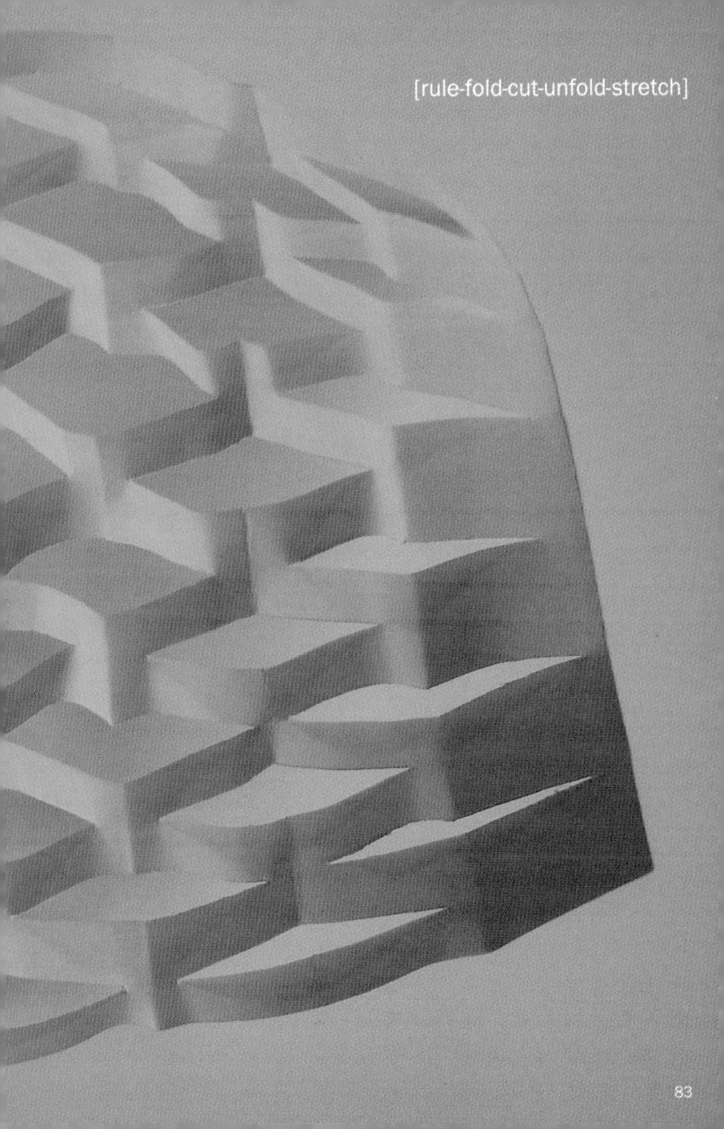
[rule-fold-cut-unfold-stretch]

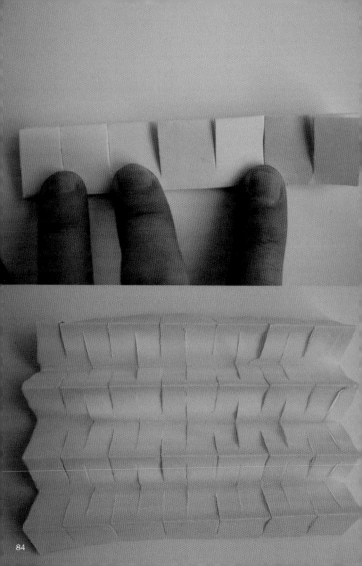

contractible roof

corrugation

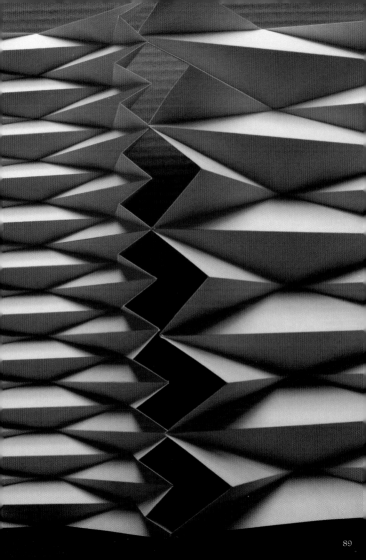

retractable membrane roof

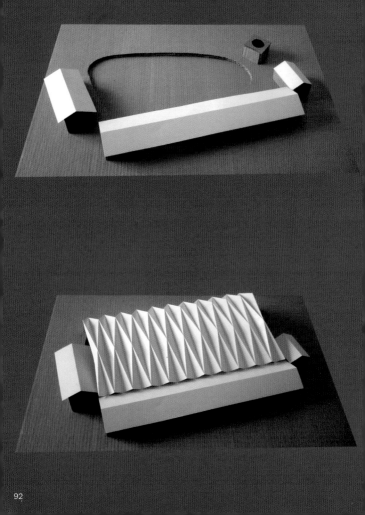

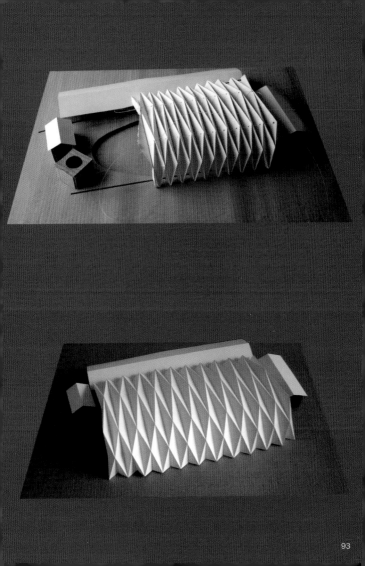

12.   kinetic truss

[score-crease-press-unfold]

paperfold deployment procedure

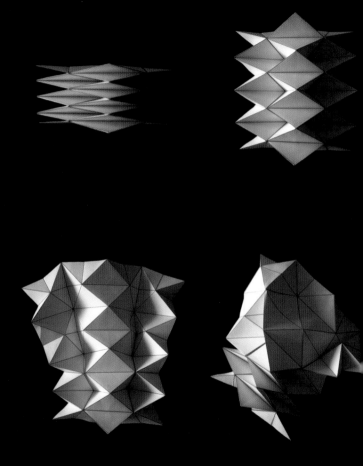

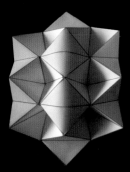

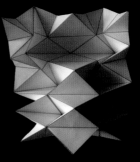

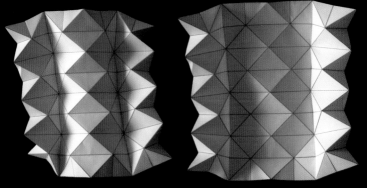

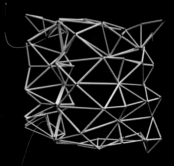

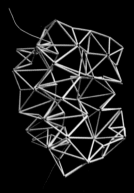

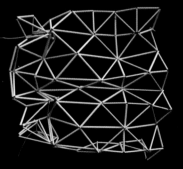
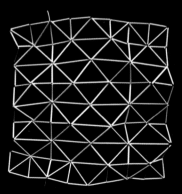

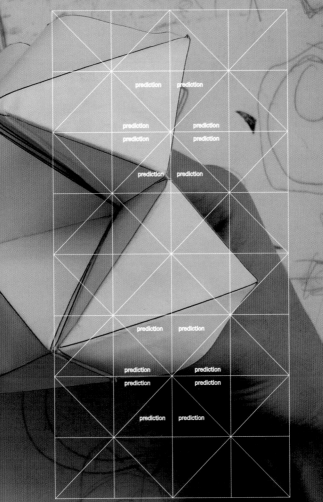

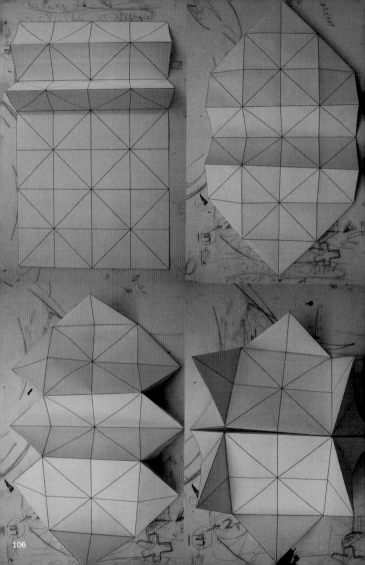

16 possibilities

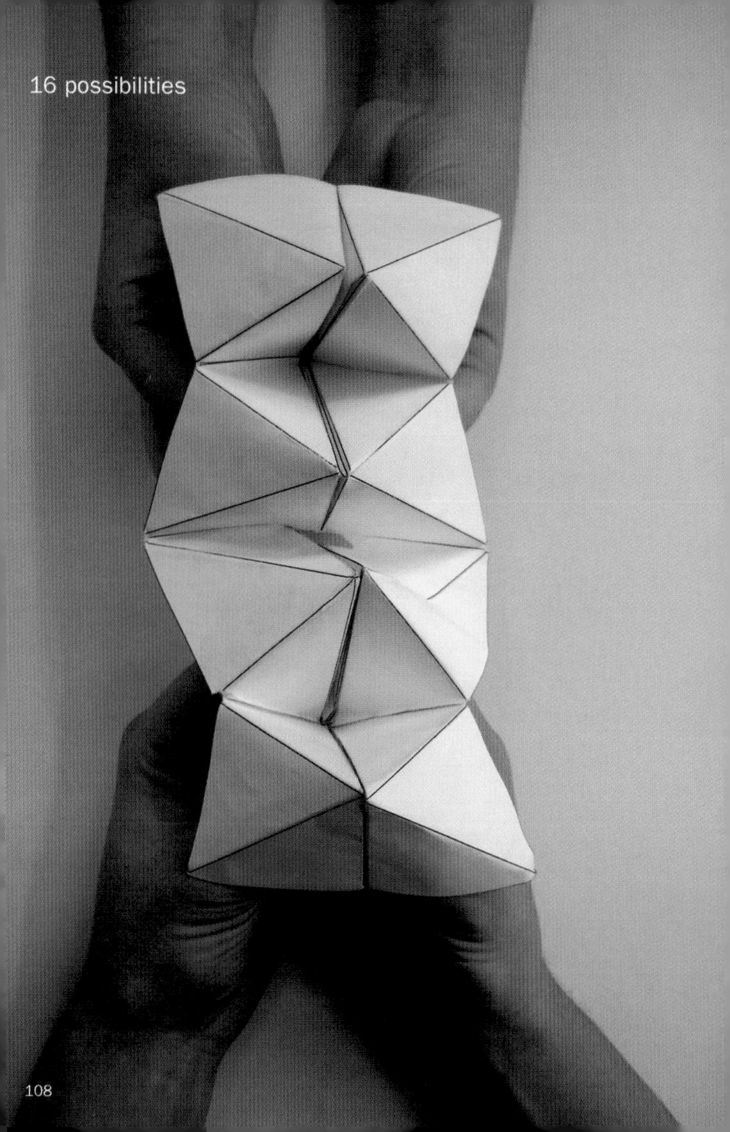

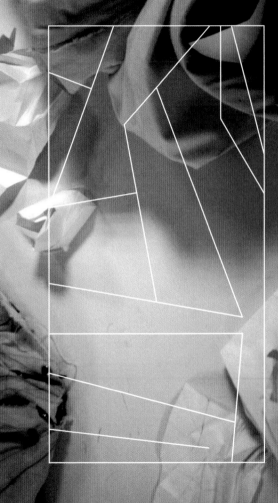

[score-crease-wrap-fix]

reinforced canvas

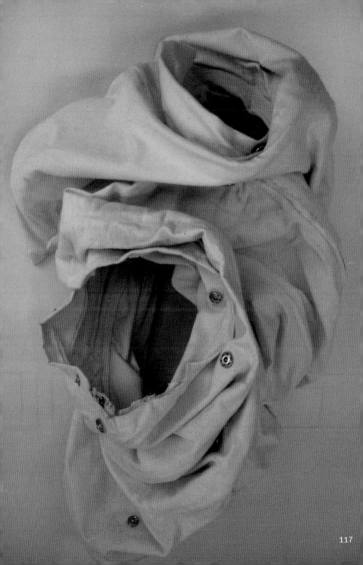

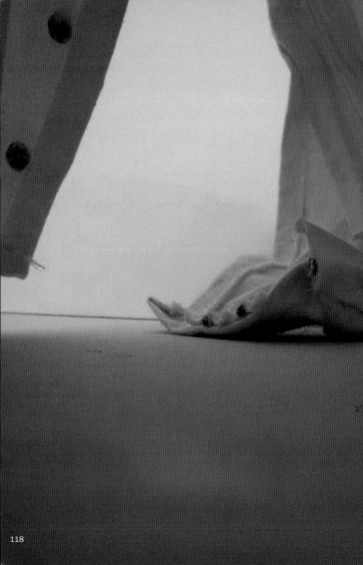

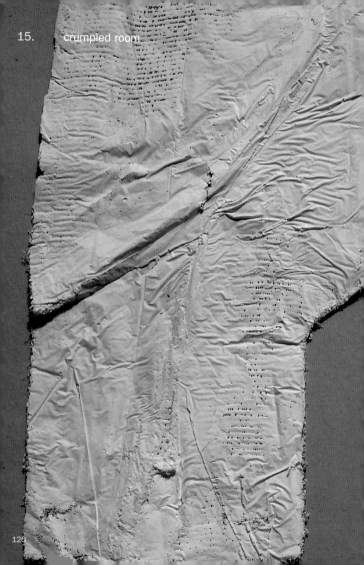

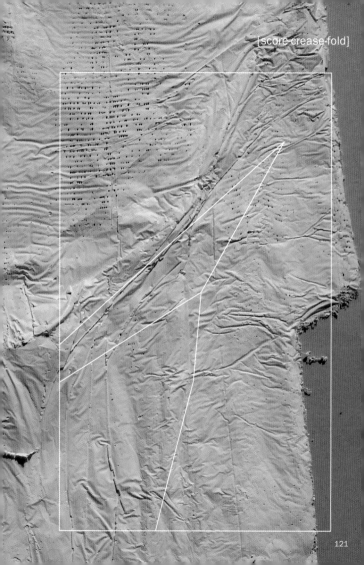

[score-crease-fold]

gypsum band

123

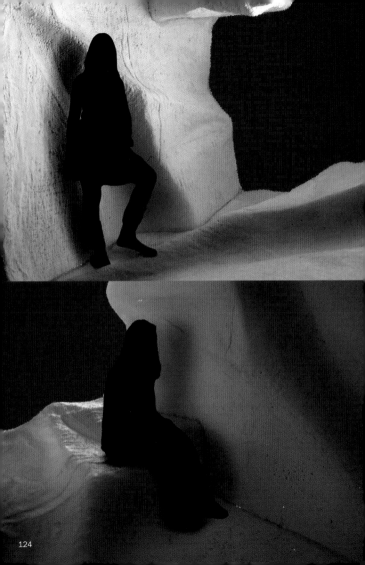

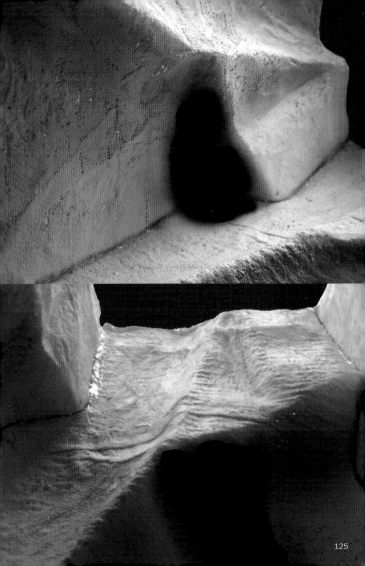

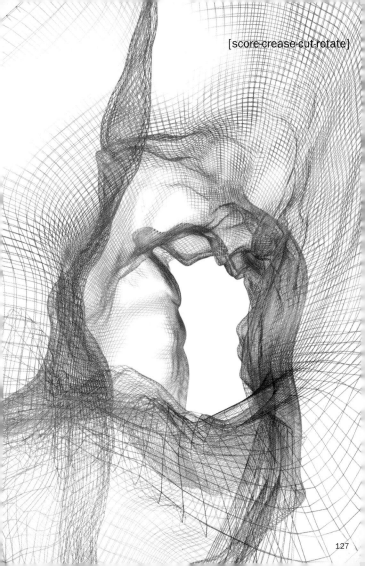

127

paper

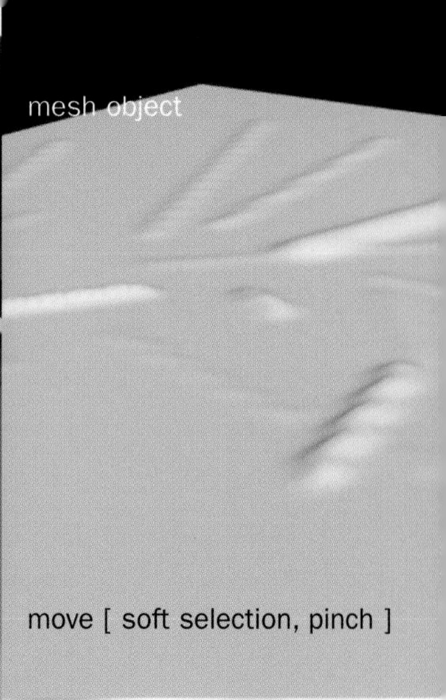

mesh object

score

move [soft selection, pinch]

cut

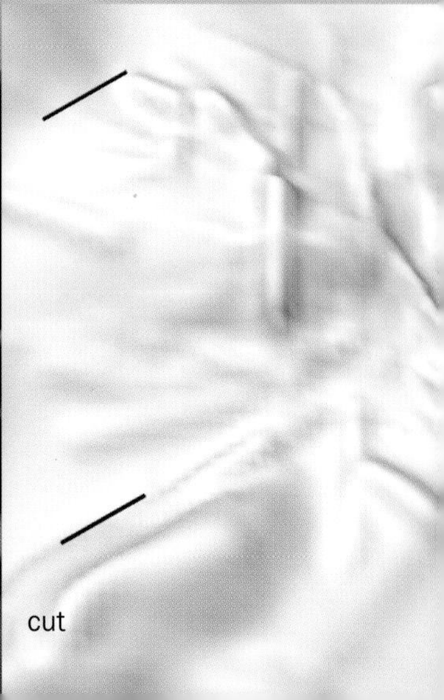

cut

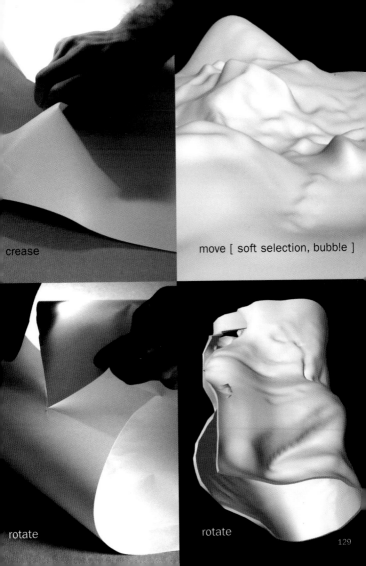

crease

move [soft selection, bubble]

rotate

rotate

129

[crumple]

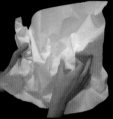

mesh

mesh & celophane

18.   paper crumpler

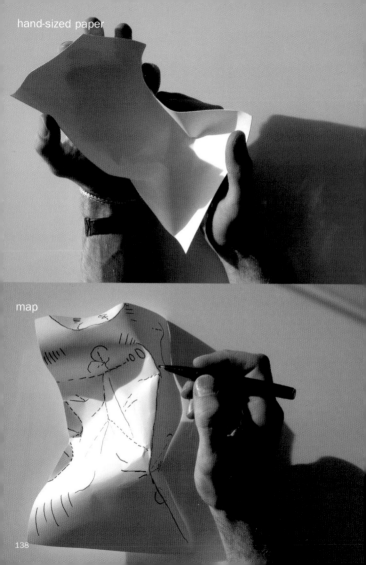

hand-sized paper

map

crumpled gesture

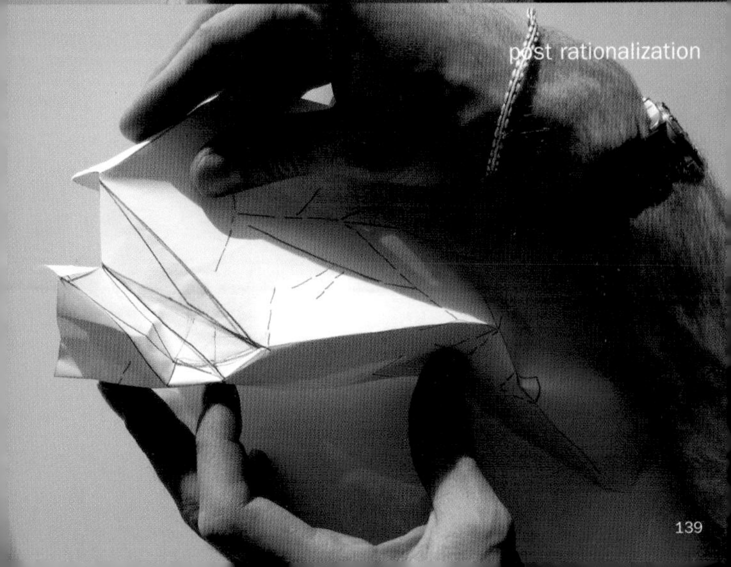

post rationalization

colophon

Text by: Sophia Vyzoviti
Design by: Sophia Vyzoviti, Constantine Galanopoulos
Photography: Sophia Vyzoviti and the students

Project credits:
1.elastic paper band: Stephanie Chen, 2005
Fold it! Workshop, Industrial Design Engineering,
Royal College of Art, UK
2.lanternette: Sophia Vyzoviti, 2005
3.twister: Fani Vambula, 2005
Folding Architecture Elective, Department of Architecture, University
of Thessaly, GR
4.porous screen: Haritini Stavroula, 2006
Supersurfaces Design Studio, Department of Architecture,
University of Thessaly, GR
5.flexichair: Manolis Iliopoulos 2005,
Folding Architecture Elective, Department of Architecture, University
of Thessaly, GR
6.body wraps: Konstandia Manthou, 2005
Folding Architecture Elective, Department of Architecture, University
of Thessaly, GR
7.body donuts: Sapho Makri, 2005
Folding Architecture Elective, Department of Architecture, University
of Thessaly, GR
8.multigarment: Sapho Makri, 2006
Supersurfaces Design Studio, Department of Architecture,
University of Thessaly, GR
9.meander chaise: Virginia Sotiraki, 2006
Supersurfaces Design Studio, Department of Architecture,
University of Thessaly, GR